# A Journey to Bulgaria

## A DAUGHTER'S PROMISE

JAYNE WETHERFIELD

Ordering Information:

Prime Seven Media
518 Landmann St.
Tomah City, WI 54660

Printed in the United States of America

# MY TRIP TO BULGARIA

# PART ONE

# LONDON TO ITALY

*I*t all started at the beginning of June 2006 with a phone call from my dad. He said that he had sold his house and was moving to Bulgaria where he had bought another house in Balchik, Dobrich County.

Dad had moved from Ireland back to the UK for reasons he never told us at the time. We often wondered if we had upset him or, did he just feel lonely and wanted to return to his friends and family who he had left behind two years previous. And now he is moving yet again and I don't know why, but I have my suspicions.

Dad moved to Ireland after his second wife left him and divorced him. They moved from Wales to Lincoln to take over a post office business and be close to his wife's mother. They had one child together, a daughter called Abigail, Abi for short. I often flew to Lincoln to see her and we became close sisters. She was in her early teens when her parents separated and divorced. Dad was very distraught and came to stay with us in Ireland and soon moved to Ireland saying he needed a new life. All went really well for two years.

Slowly dad became distant, he wanted to move back to the UK and within three months, his house was sold and he left Ireland.

My suspicions were correct, he told me that he had met another woman. But this time it was on the internet. He had first met her while he was living in Ireland and he had fallen in love with her. They wanted to get married but they couldn't marry in Ireland. That's why dad moved to the UK and after two years of his lady friend visiting the him for six weeks each visit which dad paid for in full, they wanted to get married and settle down.

However, if they had done their homework from the beginning they might have gone straight to Bulgaria, married and returned to his house in the UK and saved a lot of money. Dad also told me that she was 6 months older than me. Actually, I felt very sick hearing that.

Dad said he was making the journey to Bulgaria by road because he had all his household furniture, electrical and personal gear, garage equipment and machinery to take with him. Dad had bought a left-hand drive, 4x4 Nissan Terrano and a very large storage trailer which was attached to the tow bar of the jeep. The jeep was also packed full of bedding, clothes and his little dog. Dad asked if I would go with him for company and to share with the driving. Dad had already booked the ferry from Dover to Calais and needed my decision as soon as possible.

This was a big decision to make at such short notice and due to my commitments at home. My family, my work, my horse. I was also aware that if I said 'No' dad would have to do the journey alone. Some said it was a crazy idea, but I loved a challenge and despite all my reservations about the whole moving across Europe to another county for him to marry a woman who only wants dad's money, was not my problem. I was suddenly looking forward to probably taking on one of the toughest challenges I have ever and will ever be confronted with. My mind made up. Yes! I'm going to do it.

I didn't want to sound too eager about it and had to subdue my excitement when talking to my husband that I had decided to do this journey. Des tried to talk me out of it because he worries about me but knowing how headstrong I am, he gave up trying. I then rang dad and told him that I would do it and I would get him there safely.

Dad had to be out of his house the night before I landed at the airport. This meant he would be homeless for one night. He rang David, his eldest son (my brother) who lived close by and asked if he could stay the night due to the circumstances. However, he was refused because David's stepson was coming home from being abroad and needed the bedroom. Dad would have to sleep in the jeep for the night.

# THE JOURNEY

*F*ive days later I was on the flight to Stanstead Airport and arrived Monday night at approximately 9.30pm.

Dad met me at the arrivals and we hurried out to where the jeep and trailer was parked. I was surprised when he told me that he had parked outside the airport because he was unable to manoeuvre the large vehicle and trailer anywhere other than forward. It was now dark but I could still see the full size of what was now obvious to me that only myself was going to be towing this huge storage box for the next few days. My mouth dried up as I stared at this monster of a trailer. It was white and a lot longer than my double horse box which I tow frequently around Ireland to attend my dressage shows and by the sight of how low it sat on its springs; it was packed full to the hilt. The 4x4 was a long wheelbase left-hand drive Nissan Terrano. The whole lot together looked humongous.

Dad was anxious to get going as the ferry in Dover was booked and we had a long slow journey ahead. My heart was pounding and my mind racing, "great start" I thought and cursed silently, hoping my father couldn't lip-read! We jumped in and with no time to for rehearsals, slowly moved away. I could feel the weight behind and the pressure on the clutch pedal. I wasn't confident that the jeep would make it out of England let alone get to Bulgaria. Dad had the whole route carefully marked out so all I had to do was listen and guide this monstrosity to our destination. M11, M25, M20 and finally the A20. The journey of 101miles seemed to take forever and I was exhausted already. M left hand was quite sore due to hitting it against the door looking for the gear-stick which was never there in the first place as this is a left-hand drive. We replenished the dsl tank and joined the queue for the ferry. I longed for a cup of coffee and a lie down. Then it crossed my mind whether or not I could even get as far as France if this is how I felt after the first stage.

At last, we boarded the ferry, parked up and made our way to the restaurant. After a good meal we headed for our cabin and I slept the whole hour and thirty minutes of the sailing

We arrived in Calais in the early hours of Tuesday morning and from then on it was drive a lot and sleep a little. However, we felt very rested after the ferry journey. With a pocket full of glucose sweets to keep me alert, we commenced the first part of the journey from Calais to Turin.

It was a lot easier for me now that we were travelling on the right side of the road, I felt more relaxed, although I still kept indicating with the windscreen wipers and hitting my left hand against the door trying to change the gears.

We arrived in Lille 70 miles later. I was anxious to find somewhere to park up so I could get out and stretch my legs. We soon came across a service station and filled up with fuel. I felt that my body and mind needed more energy boosts. The glucose sweets didn't feel like they were doing much to help me feel energetic enough for this massive journey. While I was inside the shop I could see plenty of cans of Red Bull (They were labelled in French but looked the same) I scooped up 10 large cans as well as ordering 2 coffee's and left them on the counter for Dad to pay! Once back in the jeep, I closed my eyes for a while, then fell into a deep sleep. I woke sometime later, the sun was glistening, dad wasn't anywhere in sight.

Had I slept too long? What was the time? I jumped up to see the clock on the dash board, it was only 8am. Dad was walking his little dog so I took off to freshen up in the wash-room. Soon we were back on the road heading for Turin.

Sipping the Red Bull as we journeyed on made me feel more alert, apparently too much of this is not good for the heart, but I needed to stay alert.

The miles passed and we chatted and gazed at the scenery which personally, I thought was quite boring. What I did find interesting was each time we stopped for a bit to eat, I could hear people talking in French and wondered what they were saying. Their food was very different to what we're used to but it was ok when you are hungry. Their coffee was delicious and the people were really friendly and helpful. I liked the French.

We travelled on for hours, dad nodding off every now and then until, 312.73 miles later plus three more loo stops and weak from tiredness, we arrived in Dijon and located a service station where we could park up for a short break. We ate a small meal and had some refreshments before I curled up on the seat in the jeep and slept soundly for two hours. Again, after a coffee and a trip to the wash room, we were on the road to Turin. I felt more comfortable driving for a full day rather than basing our rest periods on the miles travelled. We decided the only stops we would make from now on during the day would be to fill the tank, pick up food and drinks and obviously, the loo run! Stopping to sleep at night only.

187.94 miles later we arrived at Grenoble and pulled into a service station to fill up the diesel tank, find a wash room and buy some food and coffee to take away. I walked around the car park to stretch my legs and dad took his little dog to do the same. Back in the jeep, we ate our food and drank our coffee. Half hour after pulling in, we were back on the road heading toward Turin. We still had a long way to go if we wanted to be there by midnight. Our average speed so far is 45mph but this was reduced greatly when pursuing hills, sometimes even down to second gear depending on the severity of the inclines.

Finally, at half past midnight, we arrived at our destination very tired. We pulled into an all-night service station and parked up. Dad went off to get food and coffee but I was too tired to move so curled up on the seat and fell sound asleep.

Dad called me saying that we should make a move toward Bologna. It was 4.30am and I still felt very exhausted and needed more sleep, so I kindly but firmly stressed very clearly that I need more sleep and had no intention of moving my head before 7am. Nothing more was said.

I opened my eyes to brilliant sunshine…… It was 6.45am and very hot. Red Bull had attracted the mosquitos to my skin, there was a fine bite on my arm. The first of many more to come. After eating a good breakfast of sausages, rashers, eggs and toast, washed down with a mug of coffee, we began the 146.95-mile journey to Bologna.

Italy was so different compared to France, mountainous with beautiful scenery and numerous tunnels that burrowed deep into the mountains and out the other side. These gigantic hollows were created into motorways and as soon as you came out of one tunnel, there was another in front of you. The lanes seemed to be narrower inside the tunnels and it was scary when very large vehicles passed by. I hated the lorry drivers with their huge lorries, they were so inconsiderate and ignorant. The lorries had very loud air horns and the drivers seemed to enjoy setting them off as they came alongside us, and successfully frightening the life out of me. After putting up with this for many a tunnel, I pulled onto the hard shoulder and checked that everything was as it should be, lights, indicators, tyres etc. I even ripped off the GB sticker that was clearly visible on the back of the trailer. However, it didn't work and the horn-blowing continued and I was now getting angry. I remembered what my mother always said when someone was verbally abusive. "do not lower yourself to their level by doing the same" Seriously good advice, so from then on all lorry drivers who let their loud horns off, got the 'one finger'. Now that made me feel good.

The poor jeep struggled on all the uphill climbs throughout the mountainous regions and I got used to the smell of the burning clutch as we climbed in second gear. The scenery became the same for miles and there were many more miles of tunnels to come.

Eventually we arrived in Bologna, 207 miles later including quite a few stops, not only for refreshments and loo runs but time to allow the clutch to cool down which seemed like it took forever but it gave us the chance to check our route. I couldn't wait to get out of Italy, the air-horns were now irritating me so much.

Finally, we arrived in Pescara 236.35 miles later. Dad was asleep and after quite a few calls, he woke up. I needed directions out of this place. With blurry eyes dad read out the directions, but they were the wrong directions. We missed the overnight parking and ended up in the centre of Pescara town. Winding our way through the narrow streets trying to find a way out was a nightmare. It was like trying to get a juggernaut through a maze. While I was trying to get to the end of one of these many narrow streets to turn left with cars parked on both sides made it even more difficult manoeuvring around each car, leaving no more than centremetres between them. Nearly there and the last car, which was parked at the very end of the street, hampered the space that I needed to turn left. There was no way that I could leave this street without touching this vehicle, so I got out and took a quick look at how much space I have before leaving as little scratches on this car. It was an old car, about 10 years and very dirty which would help to hide any scratches accidently made by me. I jumped back in but as I was about to move, I spotted a sign on a lamp post beside me. It had three pictures in a line. The words underneath each picture were in Italian but was pretty obvious as to what it meant. The first was a large lorry with a diagonal red line through it, the next was a smaller lorry with the red line through it, the next was a bus with red line and finally a vehicle towing a trailer with a diagonal red line through it. We needed to get out of here as soon as possible. I put the gear stick into first gear and pulled away. I felt a tug and heard a ripping sound of metal behind. Obviously, we left Pescara fast, using any road that was in front of us. After about half hour of driving we came across a garage and I asked if we could park up for a few hours. We were given permission and drove to the rear of the garage, out of sight. I had trouble settling to sleep due to all that had happened but, eventually I drifted off.

About four hours later I woke up. It was 6.30am and very hot and I longed for a shower or even a bath full of bubbles so I could stretch out and relax. Instead, it was a quick wash over a small handbasin in a dingy garage loo. At least I felt a little bit better. While dad was walking his little dog, I was topping up my store with 10 more cans of energy drinks. We then had a breakfast of cheese and ham sandwiches washed down with strong coffee before returning to the jeep to check the map and then starting up and heading for Brindisi and to the ferry port. Thankfully this was the final part of the journey through Italy.

The sky was a beautiful rich pale blue and not a cloud to be seen. To me this was the best part of this country. Every now and then we could see the Adriatic Sea, it was breath-takingly beautiful.

We arrived at the ferry port in Brindisi after travelling 263.92 miles from Pescara. Dad went off to buy the ferry tickets and sort out all the paperwork with the officials while I went for a walk around the port looking at the shops and wandering around the stalls. There was quite a crowd wandering around, some buying and some doing the same as myself. I could only see a few British people; they seemed mostly Greek. The stalls were mainly run by women selling anything from hats, clothes, jewellery, bedding, net curtains, carpets, cookware and cutlery. It was so very interesting. I suddenly noticed that some of the women on the stalls were shouting and looking at me. I couldn't understand what they were saying so I turned to walk away but it was so crowded I couldn't get away from the stalls. People were saying things to me and pointing to the stalls. I began to panic and screamed for dad. A man managed to get through the crowd to me, he was British, putting his arm around my shoulder pushed through the crowd until we got to the clear space. I couldn't stop shaking with fear. The man explained "the people were not going to hurt you. They knew you were British, therefor they were encouraging you to buy some of their goods. They meant no harm" I began to calm down and thanked the stranger. I heard my dad calling me and made my way toward him. Still shaking and so happy to see him. Dad also explained why these women wanted me to buy their wares. "When there is a British person looking at there produce, they know you have money. Therefore, they encourage you to buy. These people are very vocal and persuasive but they will never hurt or threaten you. It's their way of advertising their goods to people who have money to purchase. Anyway, we have 4 hours to wait for the ferry, our only option now is to go to the nearest bar for a well-earned drink"

# PART TWO

# GREECE TO BULGARIA

We were finally in the queue, waiting to board the ferry and when we came to the ramp, two guys approached the jeep to take over the boarding of our large load. Delighted, I jumped out and we were both told to walk the rest of the way up the ramp to a safety stand and wait for the keys when our driver had completed the parking. One of the guys jumped in behind the wheel, then after a few minutes got back out. The two conversed for a short while and then beckoned me over. They asked if I minded driving it on with the assistance of one of them directing me by walking in front of the vehicle. I tried to keep a straight face but failed and giggled all the way onto the ferry. Obviously, they weren't impressed by that.

The next sixteen hours were total luxury. The food was so delicious that I ate more than I should have. The seats were divine, soft and big enough to relax the whole, tired body. I then fell asleep for the rest of the journey and only to be awakened by the roar of the engines reversing back into the ferry port of Patrai. We are now in Greece.

We disembarked at 9am and made our way out of the port where we then headed for Ioannina. The weather wasn't quite as warm or sunny as it was in Italy which made the journey more comfortable.

Again, dad checked the map for directions and then said "we have to be in Balchik to collect the keys at 9pm tomorrow night" Balchik is the far end of Bulgaria when travelling from Greece. We had 36 hours to get across Greece and Bulgaria.

Was it possible? Well, emergency stops only for as little time as possible. Seems pretty straight forward in theory. We began the journey across Greece.

We arrived in Ioannina, 141.26 miles later and stopped for food, coffee and loo. Then onwards to Petrich.

The road began to climb and again we were down to second gear but unlike the hills in Italy, this one seemed never ending. The higher we climbed, the scarier it became. It was a mountain that we were climbing but instead of going straight up the mountain, we went around it, climbing gradually. I noticed that there were no barriers to protect vehicles from going over the edge. This was really scary. I straightened my back in the seat and just looked ahead, studying my distance between us and the edge of the road. I remembered my words to dad when I made up my mind to do this journey "I'll get you there safely"

Eventually we reached the top and we were now starting to descend. This was even more scary as not only did I have to stay in second gear but continuously and gently apply the brakes due to the weight of the trailer which wanted to push us as fast as possible and in a straight line to the bottom of the mountain.

I couldn't help glancing over the edge every now and again and very often saw vehicles in the bushes below, lorries, vans and cars that had toppled over the edge. Some had been there for quite some time as they were covered in rust. Many looked like they had recently gone over. I was really nervous now but couldn't let this affect my judgement or concentration. Dad looked pale and worried so I chatted away about various things and asking him questions about anything that I could think of at that moment. It kept his mind tuned in to me and kept mine occupied. Eventually, we arrived at the bottom of the mountain and continued on to Petrich.

We stopped at a garage near Thessaloniki for fuel. I was exhausted, hungry and my body ached but we had to try and get into Bulgaria before we rest up. We bought some strange looking food and two strong coffees. We walked around to get the blood flowing in our legs and after a short break we journeyed on. Eventually, after travelling 244.01 miles, we arrived at the border of Bulgaria.

This was a nightmare. It took over an hour sorting out paperwork and checking us out. I felt like I was in Russia during the war. Nobody smiled, they spoke frightingly stern and loud and the tension could be felt in the air. All the custom officers as well as the police carried guns. I didn't like sitting in the jeep alone but had no choice so I sat back and closed my eyes. Picturing my beautiful dressage horse back home in her field peacefully grazing and how much I longed to be there riding her. I hadn't realised that I had fallen asleep until dad jumped in and banged the door shut. "Come on, wake up, lets get out of here" he roared. He sounded very angry and said that he felt the Bulgarian officials on the border bribed him out of so much money due to the fact that he could not understand the language. They were also armed with guns which is very intimidating to Europeans.

We entered into Bulgaria and found the road to Petrich. But we needed a service station or garage to park up and rest but there was nothing for miles and neither was there any street lights as it was early hours of the morning and pitch dark. The roads were rough and full of potholes. Patience was beginning to get very thin. We had to stop somewhere, anywhere. We finally pulled off the road and into a lay-by. It was dark and eerie but I was so exhausted I would have slept on the dash-board. It was after 1am when I closed my eyes. I slept soundly until 7am and still had trouble opening my eyes. My body was stiff and I ached all over. I would have loved a shower right now but all I had were baby wipes. I wiped my face and neck; they were cold and helped wake me up a bit more. I found a bottle of water under the seat, then pulled my tooth brush and toothpaste out of my rucksack and went outside to clean my teeth. I then brushed my hair. I felt a lot better now so went for a 15-minute walk and jog up and down the road before getting back behind the wheel. Dad was studying the directions and decided to alter the route. He had found a shorter route from Petrich to pick up the main highway to Vellingrad, saving us about ten miles.

At 8am we pulled onto the road and headed toward Petrich and it wasn't long before we arrived there. Twenty minutes later we found the turn taking us to the short-cut. We travelled for about six miles before the road began to deteriorate. We thought it would improve after a while; we were so wrong. The road just disappeared into a mass of pot holes and became so narrow that we couldn't even turn around to go back, therefore, we had to wind our way onwards in first gear and sometimes, if we were lucky, managed second gear. This went on for the best part of eighty miles.

It was almost 4pm before our nightmare of a journey was over and we came onto the short-cut road. We had about twenty miles more before we arrived at the main highway but we also needed to stop for the loo run, food coffee and fuel for the tank. We pulled into a carpark where there was a small café and went in, sat down and had a good meal. Feeling better, we headed out on-route to Vellingrad.

The pressure was now building up. It was 6pm and we had two hours to get to Balchik and meet the agent who holds the keys. There was no more stopping unless it's an emergency. Soon we arrived in Vellingrad 106.83 miles from Petrich, hours later than it should have taken and we still had over three hundred miles to go.

From Vellingrad, we had to head for Stara Zagora which is 113.74 miles away. But we still had 35 miles before arriving at the main highway.

I sped off, not sparing the jeep any mercy. It had to work a lot harder from now on. Arriving at the highway, I yelled for directions and got them well in advance of reaching the junctions so there was no need to stop for anything except passing traffic. We were now on a fast road and I pushed the jeep to it's limits. Thank heavens this side of Bulgaria is fairly flat, so far anyway. I managed an average of 55mph but I wanted more. It seemed like an eternity getting to Stara Zagora and we didn't stop, driving straight through it heading for Burgas which was a further 109.17 miles ahead of us.

Dad had to make a call to the agent, letting him know that we are in the country but due to many hold-ups we will be late collecting the keys and could he possibly try and wait for us. The agent to go to his house in Kavarna where he will hand over the keys. He said that it cannot be any later than midnight. He then gave dad directions to his house.

I managed to get the speed up to 60mph and prayed that I didn't have to break hard for anyone or anything because I would never succeed in stopping without lock, stock and trailer landing in the front seat with us.

I gave up looking at my watch from then on and told dad to do same as I was under enough pressure. The road was brilliant, flat and fast. Thankfully I didn't have to drive into Burgas, the road by-passed it, although there was a sweeping bend which contained link roads. This slowed me down a little while I quickly assessed which one was mine to take and when I saw it, my foot went down on the accelerator as I smoothly steered off the sweeping junction and back onto the main road to Balchik. We had 104.35 miles to do and I was now doing just over 60mph. My mind was blank on everything except to drive as fast as possible as well as watching out for any dangers lurking ahead. We eventually arrived into Balchik and drove straight through it for the 13 miles to Kavarna, Dad rang the agent, he was not a happy man, but after a lot of persuasion and 100levs, the agent agreed to get out of bed and hand the keys over. A few minutes later, we arrived at his house and dad signed for the keys. Dad gave him the money that he had promised and we slowly drove away.

We both looked at our watches, it was 12.45am. I needed a loo run urgently.

| | |
|---|---|
| Total miles from France to Brindisi-: | 1481.91 |
| Total miles from Greece to Bulgaria-: | 832.51 |
| Overall distance travelled-: | 2314.42 Miles |

# PART THREE

## "TRAPPED in BULGARIA"

### (1)

We finally arrived at dad's new house and pulled into the drive. It was a strange looking house, a single storey on stilts. I was too tired to study it any more. The design seemed very Swiss but all I wanted now was to sleep. We didn't take very much in, just a sleeping bag and pillow case.

We climbed the steps to enter the house. inside was cold and smelt stale. I could see two bedrooms to the left of the hall, both with doors opening out onto verandas. At the end of the hall, opposite the second bedroom was a toilet. In the middle of the hall, on the right, was another hallway. There was a doorway on the right of this hall which appeared to be the sitting room. Further along the hall there were two steps rising up and just after the steps there was a bathroom to the left then straight ahead on the left was a small kitchen. Ahead of the kitchen was another room, a large room which I believed to be the dining room. There was a door at the other end of the dining room that opened onto another veranda. There was no division wall between the dining room and sitting room just two steps leading down from the dining room.

There was a large couch in the dining room and a smaller one in the sitting room which was the one I chose to sit on. There was a single bed in one of the bedrooms and dad chose that room as his. Gabby, dads' little dog had her basket alongside dads' bed

It wasn't long before we realised there was no power or water supply on due to the house being empty for so long and now it's Saturday, we won't have any until Monday at least. Our plan for tea and toast was not going to happen. We went out to the jeep and searched for bottled drink and whiskey. Fortunately, we found 7up, whiskey and a strong torch. We headed back into the house. After a couple of glasses and a long chat about the journey we bid each other good-night and headed off to our beds.

I woke to bright sunshine coming through the curtains. My eyes stung with the brightness, I tried to open them but they just felt like sand paper due to the bright light so I just closed them again and went back to sleep.

I woke to loud clattering and banging coming from the kitchen. It was dad unpacking all the kitchen ware. I needed to freshen up and my hair needed a wash but as we're still without water and electric, my shower is not going to happen. Hopefully it will all be back on by tomorrow. I rummaged around in my rucksack and found my facewipes. At least I won't be too smelly if we get visitors.

As if things couldn't get worse, If the water is off then the dungy will be out of action. I had to think of how not to fill my bladder. This was my plan…. only drink tiny sips of water all day and only eat tiny bits of food every meal time. This was not going to be easy because I was already starving. Anyway, I was going home tomorrow and it couldn't come quick enough.

However, I was looking forward to spending the day helping dad unload the jeep and container, so the sooner I get out of bed the sooner we can get it done.

I suddenly realised that I had been scratching the back of my knee more than normal but I couldn't stop. The more I scratched the more it itched. Damn these heat-bumps. But it didn't stop me snuggling back down into my sleeping bag for just another five minutes thinking about the day ahead. My arm started to itch so I began to I scratch it. Then my back itched and then my other arm. I looked down and saw to swollen red blotches on my arm and they were so itchy. Then my other leg began to itch and behind my shoulder. I had to try and stop scratching. I lay still for a few seconds. I could feel things crawling on my skin. There were things in my sleeping bag crawling all over me and eating my body. They had to come in from the couch that I was sleeping on. The couch was crawling with something and my guess was, fleas and they weren't hungry anymore after eating into my flesh and drinking my blood. Thank heavens dad always had flea powder for his little dog but, where is it. I had brought with me insect 'bite & sting' relief roll-on and smeared plenty of it all over my body.

It was a hot day; the sky was a beautiful clear baby blue with a bright yellow sun streaming down. It was the right time to put the sleeping bags over the line. I then went in search of the flea powder. I eventually found it and dowsed every part of the couch, underneath, the seating and in every corner and went to dads' room and smothered the mattress with the powder. Then I went out to the line and covered the sleeping bags inside and out with flea powder.

I was so looking forward to opening the trailer and seeing what was in it that was so heavy to pull but first we unpacked the jeep which contained boxes of food, kitchen utensils, crockery, pots, pans, bedding, bathroom toiletries etc. And not forgetting Gabby's (dads' little dog) storage box containing her blankets, toys and food.

We finally got to the container and dad opened the back door and lowered the ramp. Everything was covered over with blankets and sheets. The first item we unloaded was a standard size freezer, next a fridge of the same size and behind was a single size mattress which I managed myself while dad managed to gather up all the bedding used to cover items. There were a few other heavy items, a washing machine, microwave, Dyson hoover, large flat screen TV, small TV. That was all the household items. Then we began to remove the garage tools and equipment which was mostly woodworking heavy duty DIY tools such as a bench drill, floor-standing circular, plainer, lathe. Then the smaller tools, wheelbarrow, a wooden horse. Finally, it was the last item on the trailer was dads' motorcycle scooter.

We unhitched the empty container and pushed it into the corner of the driveway. It was now evening and still very hot.

We were thirsty and extremely hungry however, finding somewhere to eat out shouldn't be that hard because we saw plenty of restaurants on the roadside every few miles.

We stopped at the first one that we came to and after parking at the front of the restaurant, we strolled in. There was nobody else in there so we chose the best seat nearest the bar. The menu was on the table and we opened it but nothing was in English but there were pictures of each dish and every one of them looked delicious. We both picked the chicken meal and in no time at all, the waiter arrived. Apparently, there is only one person who does everything in these roadside restaurants and that person is the cook, the waiter and barman and they don't speak very much English.

He stood tall alongside our table and spoke in Bulgarian. We guessed he was asking us what we would like. We pointed to the meal that we wanted and ordered to pints of beer. It took a little while to describe the drinks that we wanted but I think he eventually understood because he came back with two glasses of beer or lager, however, it was the best tasting beer I have ever had.

The waiter had a very cold and had a stern face, he never once smiled and I felt that he was more Russian than Bulgarian. When he spoke, he sounded like he was giving us an order. He eventually left for the kitchen.

We talked endlessly about various things until our meal arrived. We were so hungry and looked forward to eating our food. The waiter put our food on the table and left. We just stared at the food; it was nothing like the picture on the menu. We were full sure we had ordered baked potatoes and beef stew. In a deep dish we could see stuffed large peppers in a watery gravy with bits of white meat, chicken skin and a chicken claw. We couldn't even bring ourselves to try it. We had never seen such a mess of food like this before. We paid and left.

We found a grocery on route back to dads and it was open. We parked up and went in. We bought as much as we could recognise, bread, butter, ham, cheese and mustard. We also bought a couple of bottles of water and a bottle of vodka.

We arrived back to dads and made lots of the best tasting sandwiches ever and washed down with water that had never tasted so good.

After bringing in the sleeping bags off the line, we had a couple of glasses of vodka and lemonade we talked and laughed for hours until I could barely keep my eyes open. Dad was also very tired so we said 'goodnight' and went off to our beds.

The following morning seemed to be warmer than yesterday. I jumped out of bed, dressed and ran outside. The garden was very overgrown with weeds and the boundary mesh fencing needed attention as it was all bent and sagging easily allowing trespassers. I really liked the style at the back of the house. The two bedrooms had outer doors that opened onto a veranda with steps that lead down to the back garden. I walked along the path that took me to the side of the house and there was a large window high above me that belonged to the sitting room. Further along was another veranda and a medium size window that belonged to the dining room and faced out onto the veranda. Alongside the window there was a door that opened out.

I carried on walking until I came to the front of the house. It was protruding toward the road, high and proud and held up by two large concrete pillars and a window almost as large as the front of the house with shutters that were bolted back against the wall. Again, I walked on toward the back end of the house. This is where the driveway comes in from the road. The gate is the old type, wrought iron and very wide. Dad always kept it closed and padlocked. The driveway passed along the back of the house toward the large garage and workshop which are joined to the house. There are three more windows on this side of the house. The largest one is the kitchen, the middle size one is the bathroom and the smallest belongs to the toilet.

I went back inside the house where the air was cooler as I was not used to this immense heat. I wondered where dad was as he wasn't in the house and not in the garage but I knew he couldn't be too far away and would turn up soon. I busied myself sorting out sorting out boxes and finding homes for the contents.

About an hour later dad called me outside. He took me to a small concrete shed, he opened the door and said "This is our temporary toilet. It was the best I could do, what do you think?" Along the back wall dad had made a completely enclosed wooden frame with an oval opening on the top and sandpapered smooth. In the centre of the front panel was a separate piece that had been cut out and replaced with two hinges on the right side and a small latch on the left, it was a little door. I opened it and inside was a bucket. "Oh dad, that's brilliant. I was debating going to the pub on the square to use their dungy which is a hole in the ground but now at last we're independent again. Your brilliant dad, thanks"

The following morning dad made a couple of phone calls to get the water and electric connected. By lunchtime we had water and by mid-afternoon the electric came on.

My flight home is at 8pm but I have to be there two hours early for check-in. Not being a regular airport traveller, I'm not sure if check-in meant passport security or just checking in luggage and with the language barrier I needed to be on the "safe-side" so to speak. As we did not quite know how long it would take us to get to Varna airport, we decided to leave at 4pm, giving us plenty of time to sit and have a cup of tea together.

We left on time and I drove. The road was quiet all the way and we arrived an hour before the check-in time. Dad wanted to leave straight away while it was daylight as he hadn't done much driving on the right side of the road since arriving in Bulgaria. He apologised for not staying for tea. We hugged and dad left. I wandered the airport, in and out of the shops but I didn't have much money on me, just enough for a coffee or tea and maybe a little more to buy food on the flight.

Soon it was time to find the check-in and headed up the stairs to security. There was no queue thankfully. I'm either very early or everyone else went through much earlier. I handed my passport to the security guy who checked it on his monitor. Why are Bulgarians so serious, why don't they ever smile, talk or even or even answer when spoken to. I don't know but I do know that this guy is taking a long time with my passport. He eventually turned and glared at me, then in a loud, frightening roar shouted, "WHERE IS VEHICLE?" I froze with fright and for a moment couldn't speak and just stared at him in shock. He repeated these words in a much louder and in a more aggressive tone. I suddenly realised that he meant dad's jeep. I replied in a very shaking voice "It's my fathers jeep and he has it in his new home in Batovo" But he kept shouting the same words over and over. I am now shaking with fear and trying to explain that it's not mine, but he wouldn't listen to me. Suddenly a very large security woman arrived and came straight towards me grabbing my upper left arm and began marching me back to the stairs. I'm now struggling to hang on to my little suitcase in my other hand. She was so rough that I bumped into the corner of walls and hand-rails as she rushed me down the stairs. I hit something at the bottom of the stairs and the pain shot through my right thigh but there was no way she cared about my pain and kept pulling me along so fast that I had to watch I didn't hit against anything else or falling altogether.

As we were passing all the queues for check-in, I saw the line for Ireland and I began to cry. People glanced at me and probably thought I was a drug smuggler. I felt so embarrassed and ashamed because I actually did feel like a criminal and I was caught and now I'm being dragged to jail.

Eventually we arrived at a small room where two armed policemen stood and both holding riffles. There was a table in the centre of the room with two chairs, one each side.

The security woman pushed me inside and pulled the door shut. I sat down and stayed very still, avoiding any eye contact with the two-armed cops. My mind was racing……. what have I done? What is wrong with dad's jeep. He had bought the jeep about three weeks before leaving England. Did he purchase a stolen vehicle and now it's been tracked to this country? Well that answers my question. I could be thrown into jail and because of the language barrier, I can't defend myself and I could be there for probably up to 10 years before I'll see my family again. I began to cry uncontrollably.

The door opened and another fully armed policeman came in. He shouted "WHERE IS VEHICLE". Again, I explained that it isn't mine but he took no notice. I pleaded with him "Please let me go home, I just want to go home". He lunged towards me and roared "YOU GO NO-WHERE, YOU

STAY HERE" He pulled me up off the seat and led me to the door, opened it and led me out. He then went back in and shut the door

I had to do something to get out of the airport and back to safety. I needed to contact dad but only had a little credit left in my phone but enough to make the call, but there was no answer. I tried a few more times but he must have put it on silent while driving. I felt so alone and frightened. The airport was full of tourists rushing to their check-ins and looking forward to their holiday. Then there are the tourists who have just flown in and about to enjoy their stay in this retched country.

I only had five euros and some loose change on me but would that be enough to ring home? The public telephones appear to only take cards that can be purchased in the airport. I went to the information desk, where a stern-faced middle-aged woman and asked for a telephone card and hoped she could speak English. She just pointed to another desk. Every noticeboard, adverts, and advice leaflets were in Bulgarian language only which made even the simplest requests hard work and time consuming.

Bulgarians are not interested in speaking English which is so frustrating. I arrived at the desk and there was another stern faced, dark haired, skinny person sat. I asked for an international telephone card and he replied in a very unfriendly voice, "sixty Lev". I told him that I didn't have any Lev only Euro's. He then shouted "Twenty Euro" I pretended to search, busily, hunting through my bag and hoping he would take pity and let me have it for nothing but of course, being a Bulgarian there was no chance of that happening. I brought out my five euro note and held it up, "I only have five euro's" He looked under his desk and brought out another card and gave it to me then snatched the five euro from me.

I quickly made my way to the nearest public telephone and rang home. Des answered and I blurted everything out as quickly and clearly as I could. I also told him that I would be cut off soon. He wanted the phone number that I was ringing from but I couldn't find it on or around the phone. Suddenly the phone went dead.

I felt better now, knowing my family is aware of what is happening here and I also knew that they would fight tooth and nail to get me home.

Now I need to get to Batovo but I have no money. Maybe if I could find a coach going to Albena Holiday Resort and promising to pay when we get there, would they trust my word. I tried dad's number again but still no answer and my battery will be flat soon. The thought of being left in this airport all night alone terrified me. I sat down and cried, I was so alone and afraid.

I thought of my family, my husband Des, my two sons Liam and Declan (Decy) and my sister Jonty. My beautiful horse Pepsi, my two dogs Budd and Judy, my job and my friends. Again, I cried quietly but still uncontrollably.

Sometime later I felt a tap on my shoulder. I looked up..." Are you ok love?" The lovely sound of an English voice seemed to make my heart beat normal again. He was about mid-fifties, small build and short with a kind look on his face. He was wearing a black three-piece suit and introduced himself as John and asked why I was upset and could he help. He sat down beside me and listened while I poured out all that had happened. When I had finished, he told me that he was one of the tourist agents and there was a coach leaving in about ten minutes carrying a party of Irish holiday makers to the

Albena Holiday Resort. John then said that he will talk to nicely to the driver about taking me, free of charge to Albena where I could get a taxi to my father in Batovo. I thanked him so much and then waited anxiously.

A short time later, a burley chap headed toward me and beckoned me to the exit door. He introduced himself as Anton the driver of the coach going to Albena and beckoned me to follow him. We passed many coaches before arriving to the one he was taking to Albena. He had also saved the front seat for me.

I felt like a penniless vagrant but it didn't bother me too much because I was out of the airport and soon heading toward Batovo. My only concern was that I get there safely. I looked at my watch for the first time since making my way to the passport security in the airport and was surprised at how fast the time has flown as it is now 3am.

It seemed to take longer by coach and of course it's dark, but I didn't care, just as long as we were heading for Albena. It's so strange listening to the Irish tourists singing their hearts out and not a care in the world. Some of them might not live too far away from me in Ireland, but what if one of them is my neighbour? I turned my head toward the window, out of sight. I reflected over all that had happened in such a short time and realised at this time I would have been in Luton airport, happy and looking forward to my flight home in Ireland. There was a strange noise coming from underneath the coach. It got louder and louder, one by one the tourists stopped singing. We were travelling along a very dark narrow road. The coach was slowing down and there was a strange smell, like something was very hot yet not a burning smell. Anton had to try and keep the coach going until he found a safe place to pull in. Soon we came to a lay-by and pulled in and Anton turned the engine off. He then proceeded to get everyone off safely. It was over an hour before the relief coach arrived and the Irish tourists cheered with joy. They were tired and cold and longed for their bed. It was 5am when we arrived in Albena and Anton stopped just before the turning for the Holiday Resort. He showed me where the taxi rank was but suddenly decided to come with me and talk to the driver. Anton had very little English but made it clear to me that he didn't trust taxi drivers. As soon as we got to the taxi, Anton had a very heated talk to the driver who he instructed to take this lady to her father's house in Batovo. Anton then turned to me and said "This man takes you to Batovo for free and I say to take care, for no harm come to you and he say yes" I shook Anton's hand and thanked him dearly.

We soon arrived at dad's house which was in total darkness. The driver asked if I would be ok on my own or should he accompany me to the door. I thanked him and said that I will be fine. I took out my purse and emptied all the change I had and gave it to him. I then got out and pulled my suitcase out with me and made my way to the gate, and along the path to the steps up to the door. I pulled on the door-handle but it was locked. Dad must be in bed as it is still very early. I knocked and called but there was no sound. I knew then that dad was not at home. Did he know that I am in trouble and is he out looking for me or didn't he arrive home at all after dropping me at the airport. Something made me wonder if dad ever left a spare key around. I began to look around, under plant pots, behind stones, under the doormat and yes, there it was. Thank you, dad, I said to myself and unlocked the door and went in. I put the key into another secret place. I went into the dining room sat at the table wondering why dad wasn't here and suddenly the whole day's events came flooding back and I began to cry uncontrollably. It was 6am, daylight was breaking and people were walking down the road on their way to work. At this time in the morning, I should be leaving the hotel in Luton, which was walking distance from the airport, and making my way to the airport departures. Instead, I have to face it, I'm trapped in Bulgaria and wondering whether I'll ever get home to my family. I went to the drinks cabinet and poured myself a large vodka and lemonade in the hopes that it would cheer me up and make me feel that little bit better. I then plugged my phone into the charger and sat down.

# THE CALL

What had happened when dad left me at the airport and arrived home around 7pm. He had something to eat and went to bed. His phone rang about 2am and it was Des. He told dad that I had not made the flight and I was in trouble, briefly explaining what had happened and that I was now being driven to Albena on a coach.

Dad was worried not knowing where I was. He drove to Albena and waited for hours, checking every coach that was due in so that he could be there when I arrived. But somehow, he missed me. He made his way back home at 7am not knowing what to do next. He eventually arrived back home and was surprised and relieved to see me home safe and sound. I explained everything that had happened and dad was shocked. But most of all, having me home safe was all that mattered for now. I could hardly keep my eyes open as I was so tired. I pulled out my sleeping bag and curled up inside it on the couch.

I woke later that morning and heard a lot of talking going on in the kitchen. I still felt very tired and just wanted to stay asleep. But I managed to drag my tired body out of the sleeping bag. I checked my phone, it was 10.15am which meant that I had only slept for two hours at the most. I headed for the kitchen where the voices were coming from. It sounded like a room full of women from the volume of chattering going on but there was only two women. We all greeted each other and dad introduced Bridget and Amy to me, then introduced me to them. The two women are mother and daughter.

I made tea for us all and we settled down to discuss what had happened. Bridget had lived in Bulgaria for many years, she and her partner, Gareth which was just a short drive from dads. It seemed like she knew quite a bit about the legal system here and advised we go to the solicitor for help and legal advice. Bridget also mentioned that once I have been given my freedom, I will then need documentation allowing me, legally, to leave Bulgaria. Bridget said that she will take me to the Governmental Buildings to have them completed as soon as I was ready.

The two women left and we decided to have a little bit to eat first before leaving for Dobrich. Dad's phone rang, it was Des. He told us to go to the police station in Dobrich as soon as we can and ask for the Detective Inspector. Des had managed to get hold of this detective through the help of an Irish Official.

We headed into Dobrich and began to search for the police station. After three stops at garages asking for directions, we eventually found the station. I felt very nervous and clung onto dad's arm. I remembered the way the airport police had treated me and I didn't feel that these would be any different. My heart was pounding and I was shaking all over. I left dad do all the talking. We were told to go upstairs, turn left and knock on the first door on the left. I was expecting a big, hard-faced middle-aged man and then to shout at us to come in. How wrong I was. The door swung open and a tall, dark-haired man, pleasant looking man, probably around the mid forties and shook our hands. He introduced himself as Marty. He had a pleasant smile and beckoned us in. He knew exactly why we were there and said that he had had a long conversation with my husband, Des who had told him everything. Marty didn't mention what had happened at the airport, how I was treated or how I had managed to get back to Bavato safely. However, he explained how I was not allowed to leave the country. It was all because I had driven dad's vehicle across the border from Greece to Bulgaria. The action had tied the vehicle to my passport making me the owner. Therefore, when I appeared at the airport control area and handed my passport in, the officer sported the vehicle details on the computer and called for another officer to re-check it. It appeared that I had maybe sold the vehicle and was trying to flee the country leaving a British Registered vehicle in Bulgaria and legally, I was violating the law which is an extremely serious, illegal action in this country. He advised us on how to undo this, which is very simple. All I had to do is to drive the vehicle across the border into Romania and then swap seats and let dad drive it back into Bulgaria. That will release the vehicle off my passport and return it to dad's passport. The Detective advised us to do it as soon as possible. We thanked him and left the station. We didn't have our passports with us and returned to dad's to collect them before setting off for Romania. However, as soon as we had returned to dad's house, he was reluctant to do the journey to free my passport. He asked me why I was in such a hurry to go home. He said that Janice, his fiancé would be arriving from Russia on Thursday and would like me to meet her. I was shocked and couldn't believe how quickly he had changed. I felt angry and upset. I needed to get home to my family, my life and my job and I told him this but he brushed it off as if it was all immaterial. We rowed over it and I told him that he was being very selfish and only thinking of himself. I also told him to be to be careful of upsetting Des and my sons Liam and Declan who are all very protective of me and not the type to put up with him trying to stop me from going home. Therefore, he had better get himself sorted immediately. Reluctantly, he agreed and soon we were on our way to Romania. It was further than I expected but eventually we arrived at the border. It was a small border, slightly dilapidated with two Romanian police controlling the passage. They checked our passports and documents and waved us through. We drove a little way in but couldn't go too far as it was getting dark and I suddenly felt very tired. We swapped seats and returned to the border. The police officer checked our passports and documents again before waving us back through to Bulgaria. I was almost free, and so looking forward to going home. Just one more bit of documentation to sort and I will then be able to leave Bulgaria.

Caroline and Bridget arrived the next morning ready to take me to the government buildings to sort out the documents but dad wasn't happy about everything happening so quickly and asked if we could leave it for a couple more days. He insisted that there was no need for me to return home so soon. Bridget could sense there was tension between dad and myself. She told dad that there was no time like the present to get this done because if we came across any problems, we had plenty of time to fix them. He had no choice but to agree once again. The three of us women left straight away before dad had a chance to argue any further.

We arrived at the government buildings. Bridget told me not to say anything, just leave it to herself and Caroline because if these officials weren't happy with a statement or answer they will refuse to allow any documentation, and I wouldn't be able to leave. I was so grateful to these women. I listened to the fast talking, but not one word of English was spoken, it was all in Bulgarian. Many questions were asked and all answered by the women. About an hour went by before it was all completed and we left the building. Bridget told me that it would normally have cost at least 50 Lev, but as the officer knew the women, he did it as a favour.

Later that evening dad and myself went out for dinner. We had found an English run restaurant a few days ago in a little village about five miles away and the food was good. For our dinner we had baked potatoes chicken and gravy, washed down with a glass of lager. We returned home very tired; it had been another long day so I went straight to bed and slept soundly. My phone rang, waking me at 10am. It was my son, Declan. He's an aircraft technician working in Germany. He told me that I was booked on the 8pm flight that evening from Varna to Gatwick and said he would ring me later with the flight details taking me from London to Ireland. I jumped out of my sleeping bag and ran out to find dad and give him the good news. He said he was delighted for me but I could see in his face that he wasn't. Dad wanted me to stay a bit longer to meet his new fiancé who was arriving the next day. But how could I stay after all that has happened to me over the past 2 says. I need to go home and I longed to be home with my family, to feel safe and secure again. I also needed to get back to work.

The day seemed endless, I needed something to keep me occupied so I can get to the late afternoon quickly and we can then leave for the airport. I could feel my insides shaking with nerves. Will I really get out of this awful country? Or will something else go wrong. I have to find something to occupy my mind. Declan has not rung me with arrangements to transfer me from Gatwick to Ireland. I wasn't too worried about it as long as I arrive in Britian. I can then find my own way to Ireland quite easily. Dad was outside working; I wonder if he'd like some help.

Bridget and Caroline called in just after lunch to check that all my documents and passport was in order. Bridget reassured me that I will be fine and on my way home without any hitches. I wish that I felt as confident. I hugged them both and thanked them dearly for what they had done for me, and they left.

Once again, I put my hand luggage into the boot of the car and we drove to Varna airport. This time dad came in and stayed with me until it was time to go to the security gates. Dad and I hugged each other before I finally went through the gates. He watched me go to the passport control and hand over my passport. My heart was pounding and I felt sick with the fear. The security officer handed back my passport. I turned, and with a big smile, I waved "GOODBYE" to dad. I made my way to the gate and sat down. I still wasn't convinced that I was completely free, even though above the exit door leading to the aircraft it had in bold letters, "BRITISH AIRWAYS". I kept looking back at the door I had come through, waiting for the Bulgarian Security woman to come and grab me again. It seemed an age before the exit doors opened and the British Airways cabin crew came in and checked our passports before sending us through the exit door and towards the aircraft. Soon all passengers, including myself were on board and waiting for take-off. I suddenly realised how relaxed I was and for the first time since that terrible experience in the Bulgarian airport a few days ago, my hip began to ache and my left arm felt sore. I shut everything out of my mind and fell asleep.

I woke to a loud noise and looking out of the little window I could see that we had just landed in Gatwick Airport. I had forgotten how much I loved the country that I was born in. As soon as I was off the aircraft, all I wanted to do was kiss the ground but being surrounded by so many people, I didn't dare do it . I passed through the customs and noticed everyone had cheerful, happy faces. I felt the weight lifting from me. There was a lump in my throat, I really wanted to cry. I wanted to cry because of all that horrific stuff that had happened in that horrid country, but also cry because I now felt so safe in my country, even though I now live in Ireland. Oh blast, I have just realised that I now need to somehow find a flight to Ireland without any money.

I made my way through customs and into the arrivals area and there, in front of me was a familiar face, it was my son Declan, waiting patiently for me. He had his usual funny grin and I could no longer hold back this lump in my throat. I hugged him so tight, the tears streaming down my face. He then said.

Let's go home Ma.

# LONDON TO IRELAND

*I* thanked Pat for accompanying Declan and we made our way to the car park, I looked up at the white fluffy clouds decorating the pale blue sky and I took a deep breath of air. it felt so good, I then put my small case into the boot of the car. Pat held the front passenger door open for me and said in his broad Irish accent, "Unless you'd prefer the back seat now Mrs". I giggled and replied, "The front seat will do me just fine thank Pat" Himself and Declan had previously arranged to meet in Rosslare and head up to an air show in Dublin today but instead, decided to come and meet me off my flight and take me home.

We left the airport car park and it wasn't long before the A23 took us to the M23. Declan knew these roads and motorways very well as he had spent months working in airports around the London region, commuting back and forth to Ireland.

Pat and Declan chatted about their days working in England and one incident in particular caught my attention as they both roared with laughter about how they beat the system.

They had been invited to a colleagues wedding but didn't have the appropriate clothing so drove into the nearest town, found a men's clothes shop, pulled up outside it and both jumped out, locking the car as they went inside the shop. After about an hour, the two returned to the car delighted with their new suits, but suddenly stopped laughing............ the car was clamped with a notice showing the cost to un-clamp and who to contact.

Declan unlocked the car and they hung up their suits, then went to the back of the car and Declan opened the boot and pat brought out a square tool box and placed it down on the pavement and opened it up. They brought out a very sophisticated looking cutting tool. Declan sat on the pavement while Pat kept watch. Declan put one leg either side of the wheel and placed his cutting tool behind the clamp. There was a loud clunk and the clamp flew open. Putting the tool box back into the boot, both lads jumped into the car and sped away. I listened to them describing their antics and tutted, shaking my head in disapproval, but picturing the two of them made me giggle quietly.

We had left the M23 and was now on the M25. Pat and Declan's chatter seemed to lull me to sleep because I woke to the sound of Declan cursing and pulling into the hard shoulder of the motorway. I sat up straight and looked around. It was dark but I could see flashing blue lights behind us.

A policeman came to my side and I opened the door. I felt very nervous and couldn't understand what was happening until he mentioned speed limits. He told Declan that there was a speed limit of 40mph due to road works and Declan had exceeded this by 50mph, travelling at a speed of 90mph and the policeman was determined to book him due to this. He asked Declan if there was anyone in Wales who could pay this fine and Declan gave the policeman my sister-in-law's address.

I felt that this was all my fault and tearfully explained to the policeman why my son had broken the speed limit, giving a short version of events which led to Declan collecting me from the airport and trying to arrive at the ferry port in time for our booking.

I think the policeman became sympathetic towards Declan and reminded him to take care on the rest of the journey. I closed my eyes and sat back in the seat. I then remembered saying those exact words to dad. "I'll get you there safely." I meant what I said and my son also means what he has said.

We finally arrive in Pembroke. My eyes felt like sand paper because I was so tired and Declan must also be extremely tired after the hours of travelling from Ireland to London and with no rest, he is travelling all the way back with only a short break on the ferry. Pat was snoring blissfully on the back seat. I hope we can find a long couch seat on the ferry so that we can lie down and sleep the whole journey. "WE'VE MISSED IT," shouted Declan. Pat jumped up off the back seat shouting all sorts of non-sensicles and still half asleep but wondering what had happened. I just glared at the ferry pulling out of the harbour, my heart sank. Declan hadn't slept since the night before and now he must be devastated and exhausted. He also stared at the outgoing ferry. We sat there for a few moments, trying to gather our thoughts. We had no choice but to book the next available ferry.

The earliest ferry was the fast ferry and Declan booked it. We then searched for a B&B and found one close to the port. It was a quaint old town house run by one person, a middle-aged man. Declan had booked three single rooms and no breakfast as we had to be out by 6am. The landlord showed us to our rooms which we had to climb up a narrow stairway to get to them. Mine was the first room which was just off a narrow bend on the stairway and he showed me into my room. Declan and Pat waited outside my door on the stairway and I could hear them talking and giggling quietly. I smiled at the landlord, desperately trying not to laugh, thanking him and bidding him goodnight.

The room was small and smelt very musky. I pulled the bedclothes back; they looked perfectly clean with no mould. There was a sink in the corner of the room and the toilet was in cupboard. The small wardrobe was at the bottom of the bed and a small chest of drawers next to it. I couldn't help but think that this is typical of a single man who has never been shown anything about the up-keep of a B&B. However, he was trying hard to earn a living. While setting my alarm on my phone, tiredness suddenly hit me hard and I just collapsed into bed.

The alarm rang loud and clear and I jumped out of bed dazed, for a split second wondered where I was. I grabbed my suitcase, pulled out my towel and other toiletries and went to the bathroom to freshen up. I then dressed and packed everything back into my suitcase. Within a short time, Declan knocked on the door and shouted "Time to go mother." I rushed to finish getting ready then left the room, closing the door and carefully went down the stairs to where Declan and Pat were waiting for me. They had both paid the bill and thanked the strange landlord. We giggled all the way to the car.

We boarded the ferry and made straight to the lounge. The ferry was very small inside but comfortable. Soon the ferry engines revved up and we began to move. Once away from the port and heading out to the sea, the engines accelerated and the ferry picked up speed. It bounced along the water so fast that it felt like it was hitting potholes all the way.

I began to feel a bit dizzy and nauseated and decided to go out on deck for some fresh air. I soon got very sea-sick so remained on deck for the rest of the journey. Declan came to my rescue when the ferry was almost in Rosslare Harbour and helped me to the car because by then, I was quite cold. Declan and Pat had slept for the whole crossing and with the colour back in Declan's cheeks, he was ready to face the final stage of this journey.

I reflected on my own journey; it's been a tough one but I'm almost there. My heart began to beat fast at the thought of seeing my husband and my sister, Jonty and hearing the dog's howling with excitement at seeing me again. Then seeing and hearing my beautiful black horse whinny when she sees me.

Again, I felt a little lump creep into my throat, but I had to dismiss it because we were now in the parking area in Rosslare Harbour and something was wrong. Pat stood beside his car in shock with both hands over his head. Declan dived out of the car and ran over to Pat; I followed close behind. His driver side window had black plastic taped all over it. Obviously, someone had broken into it. We approached the security officers and asked what had happened. Apparently, they had only noticed it this morning. Pats car was just outside the camera's view; therefore, nothing was recorded. Security cleaned up all the broken glass and taped up the window with black plastic. Pat checked all his belongings and the only thing that was missing was the bag of new clothes that he had bought for air show. Everything else was in its place in the car.

We were soon on the road out of Rosslare and heading for Wexford. Pat was following behind. It was a warm, sunny day which made the journey a lot easier. I phoned home and Des answered. "We'll be home in about three and a half hours Des, and I can't wait to see you." Des replied, "Same here my darling. I can't wait to see you. Safe home."

Passing the outskirts of Wexford, we now headed for New Ross and the traffic was getting heavy as it was now morning rush hour. We had to go through the centre of the town and it was a nightmare with traffic lights that seemed to turned red when they saw us and roundabouts that seemed to be a free for all but was now at a standstill. An hour later we began to exit New Ross, just one more roundabout and we will be heading for open road. Finally free from the hustle and bustle of morning traffic, we were heading for Waterford. Declan's phone rang on his hands-free ear-piece. He hung up almost immediately and shouted "Pat has crashed." Doing a fast U-turn, Declan headed back to the last roundabout and parked on the grass verge.

A large rental van hadn't stopped in time for the roundabout and ploughed into the back of Pat's car. Pat was physically angry, thumping his broken car and then throwing his hands up to the sky and cursing loudly. Declan ran over to him and tried to calm him down. It was a total write-off but thankfully Pat was ok, not a scratch or a bruise. The local rush hour traffic was again brought to a standstill and there's going to be a lot of late workers arriving at their place of employment today.

It wasn't long before the Gardi arrived on the scene and it took hours for all the details from both drivers as well as witnesses to be written into statements and the road measurements etc. Finally, the tow truck arrived and the traffic was moved on. Pat's car was having a very bad day today but was soon on the tow truck, strapped down and on its way to the scrap yard.

By now, Pat was pretty fed up and joined us again in Declan's car and we headed for Waterford once again. We didn't have to go into the city as there's a new ring road around it so the transition from the N25 to the N24 was driving pleasure.

On and on we travelled until we arrived in Clonmel, famous for its horse racing. Pat was still trying to work out how that lorry couldn't stop in time. Declan opened his window and pointed to the hedge that was on the other side of the road and told me not to take my eyes off of it until he said so. I asked him why, he just said "keep watching it." I laughed and looked the straight ahead in a teasing manner but then what I saw shocked and upset me so much that I found it hard to breath.

A white ford transit had mounted the curb and had gone across the grass verge, hit the wall and turned over onto the driver's side. If that wasn't bad enough, the van had been towing a horse-box with a horse on board. The horse-box was also on its side and smashed to pieces. There, lying on the grass was the most beautiful bay coloured horse which, to me, looked in perfect condition with its coat healthily shining, but the horse was dead.

That was it, my body and mind felt like giving up. When is all this going to stop. That's how I was feeling at that moment. Declan pulled into a lay-by about a mile further on from the accident. Pat got out and went for a walk. Declan held my hand and then said. "I know your upset, that's why I tried to divert your attention. I want you to take deep breaths and wipe your tears away, everything is going to be fine now. Dads waiting for us." I knew I had to get over this right now, and look forward to seeing Des. "I'm fine now Declan, and thank you. Yes, let's go home."

Declan put the car into gear and began to move but suddenly realising Pat wasn't in the car. Spotting him in the mirror, Declan rolled his window down and shouted "Hey Pat, are you coming with us or are you going to thumb home!" Pat got into the back seat and we all laughed.

We passed through many more villages and towns like Carrick-on-Suir, Cahir and, famous for its name, Tipperary. The scenery was quite breath-taking. I had never had the chance to view the green fields, hills and valleys before now because I have always been in the driving seat. Now I can see a little bit of the beauty that Ireland holds, like the rich green trees on either side of the road full of branches that appear to be laden with leaves. The mountains covered in green pasture and rising up in front of us as well as each side of us. When we left the mountainous region, we saw fields all around us. The grass looked a rich green in some fields and bright green in others and the fields were divided by hedges that were laden with a variety of different wild flowers.

"We are nearly home at last." Said Declan. And there in front of us, the big sign saying 'Welcome to County Limerick' For the first time since I was dragged about in Varna airport by that very large security woman, I feel secure, safe and confident again. I turned to Declan and said "Thank you son for bringing me home safely" I then turned to Pat and thanked him dearly for supporting Declan through the whole journey.

We arrived home and turned into the yard and the back door opened. First out was our black Labrador, Budd and our German Shepherd, Judy and they almost knocked me down with excitement, howling and licking my hands. I stroked their necks and kissed their heads. I looked up and saw Des standing in front of me. He looked so relieved to see me. A tear rolled down his cheek and he brushed it away quickly. I wanted a few seconds just to look at him. Our eyes said it all, and he put his arms around me and held me gently and securely and whispered, "I'm so proud of you and I love you so much" That dam lump came back in my throat again, my eyes were burning trying to hold back the tears but I gave in to them because I had missed Des so much and loved him with all my heart.

We went into the house and Jonty, my sister was about to pour the tea but turned around and ran to me, throwing her arms around my neck, she said "Missed you sis" I replied, "Missed you too Jonty" I replied. I suddenly noticed that Declan and Pat had disappeared and I hadn't said goodbye, but I think I would have done the same if I had been in their shoes.

There was just one more thing I had to do and I turned to Des and said "Just give me a while, I need to do something" I went out through the back door and through the garden, across the back yard and down toward the field. There she was, as beautiful as ever, my black beauty. I called "Hey Pepsi, come on girl" she looked up and neighed aloud. Pepsi made her way over to me. She lifted her head to smell my face, I kissed her nose and put my arms around her neck.

I have never appreciated what I have until this moment, but everything I love is here, all around me, and I will never take it for granted.

The End